Productivity

Enhance Your Productivity and Become the Finest
Version of Yourself to Achieve Success

*(The Ultimate Guide To Enhance Your Mental Focus And
Maximize Your Study Productivity)*

Spencer Romero

TABLE OFCONTENT

Chapter 1: Schedule Meetings Intelligently. 1

Chapter 2: Time Administration And Priority Setting... 11

Chapter 3: Maintain Responsibility 23

Chapter 4: The Word Is A Source Of Illumination. 35

Chapter 5: You Are Able To Accomplish The Unthinkable. 49

Don't Let Setbacks Depress You! 53

Chapter 6: Effective Productivity Routines 57

Chapter 1: Schedule Meetings Intelligently.

Ensure that meetings with clients, team members, and prospects are goal-oriented if you are planning them. If you spend hours per day in meetings rather than conducting actual tasks, you will be setting yourself up for a significantly longer workday.

If a meeting is necessary, you should create a realistic schedule and ensure that the discussions remain on track.

21. Color-code your calendar.

By color-coding your calendar, you can quickly determine what the upcoming week holds. It can also help you visualize your goals. Spend a few minutes assigning the correct colors to the appropriate tasks, such as red for detail-oriented tasks and green for meetings.

22. Live a life devoid of excess.

Messiness is annoying and distracting. And it is detrimental to your general health. Therefore, you must maintain a clutter-free lifestyle.

You can accomplish this by discarding, recycling, or donating anything that does not bring you pleasure or is no longer necessary. Start refusing gratuities and time demands that serve no purpose. Simplify your objectives, practice mindfulness, and avoid multitasking. In addition, schedule time to organize your desk, home, and transportation.

23. Organize like a chef

There is a French term in the culinary world known as mise-en-place. It has the meaning of "put in place." And chefs use this method to keep their facilities organized and efficient. They accomplish this by collecting and organizing all necessary culinary ingredients and equipment.

You may also apply this to your life. Ensure that every object has a home and is returned when not in use. If you need a specialized item to complete a task this week, ensure you have one before you begin working.

Nobody compares to you.

Do not engage in comparisons. It may cause you to feel awful about yourself. However, there are instances in which it can be useful. Comparing your weekly calendar or plan with that of a colleague, mentor, or productivity guru would be one such scenario. Not to make you feel small. Instead, it is an opportunity to learn how effectively they have organized their week.

Reflect and appreciate the final week

I prefer to reflect on my week's accomplishments on Friday evenings. Whether it's for achieving my goals, learning something new, or being appreciative for something, this gives me the opportunity to pat myself on the back. As a consequence, I will remain motivated to continue working.

In addition, reflecting on the past week allows me to consider what I wish I had done. The following week, I may decide to concentrate on the tasks I wish to accomplish more effectively.

Determining The Number Of Breaks You Are Permitted To Take

The number of necessary breaks can differ greatly from day to day. There will be days when you feel like you can concentrate for extended periods of time. There will be days when you feel like you can't accomplish anything no matter how hard you try.

Typically, the days when you struggle the most are also the days when you need the most pauses. When you are excessively overworked, it may be necessary to take a day off.

If you believe that you can continue working without much difficulty, you should maintain momentum for as long as possible. You must seize opportunities whenever they present themselves. You will not always feel like you have a great deal of vitality, so continue working until you feel extremely restless.

It is essential to be able to distinguish between distractions and restlessness. Inability to decide what to do can be categorized as a form of distraction. You are aware that you want to complete your primary mission, but you also have other objectives. You can still concentrate on your primary objective, but you can also concentrate on something else. In this situation, you should continue to focus on your primary objective because it is the most essential. As long as you are able to concentrate on whatever you choose, it makes sense to stick with the more essential task for the time being.

If you sense your concentration waning and you would rather be somewhere else, it is likely time to take a break. Don't waste time attempting to make something happen that isn't going to happen right now because your mind is simply not in it.

Take as many pauses as you deem necessary, but don't interrupt your progress for the sake of taking a break. If you desperately required a break, your ability to concentrate would likely suffer.

Do not use the wall clock to determine your intervals. Utilize your internal clock to determine when to take a pause.

Getting More Done Does Not Always Imply the Need for Additional Time

I used to wish I had more time to complete certain endeavors when I knew I would not be able to do so. I always had the thought, "If only I had more time." I did not recognize that my mindset at the time was incorrect. I ought not to have thought, "If only I had more time." I should have been thinking, "If only I could find a way to get more things done."

We cannot add more time to the day. There are 24 hours in a day, and that is simply the case. Complaining about the scarcity of time we have only causes us to waste more time.

Remember not to lose sight of what is genuinely significant to you. Time does not create or break a person's identity. What really matters is how you choose to invest your time. Whether you have a few hours or several decades to complete a task, every minute must matter.

If you can't slumber, get up and do something productive. Do not squander the night tossing and turning. Do not attempt to compel yourself to work if you are extremely exhausted.

Follow the current and do what you can. To be productive, you must be operating at your highest level. Therefore, you will need to engage in activities that promote optimal functioning. You must get enough sleep, eat enough food, drink enough water, breathe enough fresh air, take enough pauses, remain inspired, and maintain sufficient motivation.

You must first consider what is best for yourself, not what is best for compensation. People are most productive when they believe they are in the correct place at the right time. You must recognize the value of your labor and feel appreciated for it.

Be confident that you are acting in your own best interests. Try to unwind and conduct yourself in a laid-back manner. Believe that everything will work out for the best to reduce your tension as much as possible. Putting yourself under extreme pressure to reach deadlines is an ugly way to get things done. Desperation is not a positive trait.

It is preferable to do your best, but not at the expense of experiencing suffering. Consider your current emotional state when determining your next course of action. Adjust the situation so that everything falls into position.

Chapter 2: Time Administration And Priority Setting

It is commonly believed that time management is the "secret" to success and productivity. In theory, it sounds like a great concept, but time management is more difficult than the majority of people believe. Time management, like most of the topics in this book, requires the use of your fortitude to carry out your written plans.

Plan, Execute, Evaluate, and Repeat

There are essentially four phases to time management: (1) planning, (2) execution, (3) evaluation of completed tasks, and (4) repetition. Most people struggle with number 2, and even if they make it to number 3, the fourth portion is typically where they fail. Determine which portion of your time management cycle typically causes you difficulty and address it accordingly.

Planning Stage

When undertaking time management, most people focus on the planning phase. There is no greater pleasure than planning your future actions on paper because they appear good on paper. You convince yourself you'll complete something within a certain time frame, but it will actually take you twice as long to make a difference. Simply "promising" yourself success makes you joyful, but are you keeping your word?

Although the planning phase is not as crucial as the execution phase, it does contribute to the grand scheme of things. The planning phase includes not only what you should be doing and when you should be doing it, but also what you should do if you become distracted from what you should be doing. Anti-distraction strategies are covered in a distinct chapter of this book. Try to implement one or more of the mentioned techniques during the planning phase.

Execution Level

This is where the majority of individuals experience difficulty. An effective time management system should facilitate the execution of your plans. This portion of the activity can also make use of the techniques discussed in this book. Unfortunately, it all depends on the individual's fortitude and self-discipline.

Evaluation Period

Evaluation is an integral part of the time management procedure. It is the stage where you confront reality and determine whether or not your methods work. Which strategies work for you and which do not? Ideally, you should be able to evaluate each technique and determine whether you should continue using it or employ a different one.

Principal Time Management System Principles

Because time management systems (TMS) are so adaptable and

customizable, they can vary from person to person. Your methods may be significantly distinct from those of another individual. The plan-execute-evaluate-repeat method is therefore the only established formula.

To create an effective and readily followed time management system for your own use, you must adhere to certain principles. Here are some of these guiding principles to remember:

It Must Be Easy

The concept of simplicity incorporates an uncomplicated approach to time management. It should be clear as to what you should do and how you should do it; in principle, it should provide straightforward answers to two questions: "What should be done?" and "When should it be done?"

Therefore, the simplest method is to grab your daily planner and write down the activity you need to complete on a particular day. Complexity arises when completing a task is difficult for a variety of factors, such as (1) you don't know where to begin, (2) there are too many items that need to be addressed, or (3) you're simply too lazy to get started.

Once these obstacles begin to appear, simplicity tends to go out the window, necessitating a more inventive approach to time management. Therefore, instead of simply sitting down and beginning the task, you will need to eliminate distractions or even transfer to a different location to maintain concentration.

Therefore, a time management system begins simply before branching out into more complex conditions as you begin to implement or inculcate the habit. As a beginner, you may experience a number of false starts and pauses as you encourage yourself to continue with the "simple" layout. As you become accustomed to the routine, however, and as your self-discipline grows, the TMS can become less complicated, without the need to account for exceptional circumstances.

It Should Be Complete

Completion refers to taking into account everything that must be done in relation to the primary objective. For example, one of your subjects requires you to write a paper. The completion of the paper is the primary objective, but there are subsidiary objectives as well. Example: determining the topic of a paper, the research studies that will be used for information, and how the information will be conveyed in the paper. If you continually "refer back" to various sources while writing the paper, you will waste time by switching from one task to another.

Therefore, it is essential that the subtasks be completed prior to beginning the main task. By doing so, you will have everything necessary before proceeding to the main objective. Simply stated, you must ensure that you have all the necessary ingredients before you begin cooking. Otherwise, you may need to dash to the grocery store for eggs, milk, and other essential ingredients.

It Must Be Related.

The relationship is primarily based on completeness. In the preceding example, you must accomplish your sub-goals before pursuing the primary objective. Note, however, that having all the ingredients is not sufficient. Connection takes into consideration the establishment of order in the manner in which you perform tasks. What must be addressed initially? Which products can be delayed? Which are regarded prerequisites for a subsequent task?

It Must Be Practical

Obviously, don't neglect that your objectives must be attainable. They must be feasible within the allotted time frame; otherwise, you would be overly demanding and never complete or accomplish the task you've set.

Priority-Setting Strategies

Setting or deliberating on priorities is a crucial component of time management systems. This is rooted primarily in the planning phase and can be approached in a variety of ways. The following are some of the strategies you can employ:

ABC Analysis

This method of prioritizing duties is frequently used by businesses to manage massive amounts of data. Each division is designated as A, B, or C with categories that correspond. For instance, A assignments are those that are both urgent and significant. The B tasks are those that are significant but not imperative, whereas the C tasks are not significant. Additional classifications are possible, but for the most part, these are the fundamental task categories. To create a clearer image of how and when a task should be completed, some companies force-rank the tasks in group B to either A or C.

This type of priority assessment is most useful for domestic tasks or when working on multiple projects simultaneously. In many instances, you may find yourself reorganizing the duties as time passes. As the particular date approaches, for instance, the unimportant may abruptly become urgent and crucial. As the number of duties in the A category decreases, those in the B category may be promoted to the A category.

Pareto Analysis

The Pareto analysis is frequently used alongside the ABC analysis. This method is initially a bit perplexing, but once mastered, it is quite simple. This technique is based on the principle that 80 percent of duties can be completed in 20 percent of available time. Consequently, 20% of the duties will consume approximately 80% of your time.

The Pareto analysis requires you to divide activities into only two categories. Those that can be completed within 20 percent of your available time should have a higher priority than those that cannot.

The Pareto analysis also considers the possibility of performing a task with minimal effort. This entails discovering methods to reduce the amount of time you devote to a task without sacrificing quality.

The Pareto analysis (also known as the 80-20 rule) is somewhat more perplexing than the ABC analysis. How will you specifically apply this to ordinary life?

One thing to keep in mind is that the Pareto analysis is used to hone in on a problem and find a solution by determining the potential causes or obstacles to completing a task. Typically, the Pareto analysis is applied as follows:

A person begins by identifying the issues requiring resolution.

Each problem's fundamental cause must be identified. You can attempt listing multiple root causes.

The next stage is to assign a numerical value to each problem based on actual and quantifiable data. For instance, your problem involves determining the frequency with which consumers return products. You assign a score based on the frequency of returns. If the issue is excessive spending on a business, you can evaluate it using the money equivalent.

Due to the possibility of scoring system variations, it is perfectly acceptable to use a standard scoring system, such as a scale from 1 to 5. Nonetheless, you can also use a common scoring system by categorizing problems according to measurable data. For instance, you spend excessively on marketing, repairs, electric expenses, and food. The cost in dollars can be used to "score" each item based on the amount you're spending in excess.

After assigning a score to each problem, examine its underlying causes in detail. Important step: classify problems according to their fundamental causes. For instance, if problems 2, 5, and 8 have the same X fundamental cause, they must be grouped.

After grouping problems by their common underlying cause, the next stage is to add the scores of the newly grouped problems. The highest amount would receive top priority, followed by the second-highest, and so on.

At this stage, you have distinct problem groups with the same underlying cause. Here, the 80-20 rule becomes more apparent. By developing a solution that addresses a single fundamental cause, you will effectively be able to "solve" all the problems within a given group.

Excel allows you to conduct a Pareto analysis.

Chapter 3: Maintain Responsibility

When setting and attempting to achieve objectives, you should not underestimate the value of a trustworthy accountability partner.

You can always accomplish more when someone is by your side, providing constant support, motivation, and encouragement. Importance

Your accountability associate should be viewed as a mastermind group. They must be motivating, positive, noncompetitive, and close-knit.

When searching for the ideal partner, you must discover someone who is selfless, not someone who is only concerned with themselves. Consider a partner who benefits others without expecting anything in return. In this case, they exhibit the noncompetitive and positive pillars. You may not know whether they are cultivating a relationship by discussing your blog or business plan.

Try to choose the proper personality. Trust must be acquired over time. Before disclosing all of one's secrets, one should test the waters. You must discover someone who believes you can achieve your goals despite your current difficulties. Why Partnerships Are Vital

A partner in accountability will strengthen your "why". If you do not know your "why," you must discover it. This will enable you to visualize your goals, keep you on track, and assist you in reaching your objectives.

Once you have determined your "why," share it with your accountability partner. This will help them comprehend the rationale behind your actions. They will be better able to relate to you and to remind you of your "why" when you neglect. You may be making poor decisions by considering the "why" of others instead of your own.

They will highlight your qualities. If you have taken the time to find the right companion, you will find that they can recognize your strengths and provide encouragement.

They could assist you by having you contribute content to your website or by identifying new revenue-generating opportunities.

They can see your vulnerabilities. It won't take long to discover someone's flaws. If your accountability companion is flawless, your relationship will be secure. This implies that when your companion reveals a weakness that is holding you back, you must recognize that they are not attacking you personally, but rather attempting to help you improve.

When someone demonstrates vulnerability, they must also propose a solution. Attending a conference, enrolling in a course, or perusing a book are encouraged.

Partners in accountability must serve as reflecting boards. They are excellent for idea generation. This can only be accomplished if mutual trust and loyalty have been established.

Everyone in the universe has something they need to vent about. If you have a blog, try to keep your posts brief and avoid engaging in lengthy, negative discussions. A blog's purpose is expansion and positivity.

You must seek solutions to the issue you are venting about, or confess to your partner.

Always take the time to acknowledge your accomplishments, as they represent what is necessary and essential.

They will aid you in goal-setting. By setting objectives, accountability partners can keep you motivated.

After deciding on your objectives and taking the necessary steps to create monthly objectives, you can hold someone accountable while they hold you accountable. Create a social media group that will assist you in keeping up with your daily tasks and achieving your objectives.

They will study alongside you. When your accountability partner is attending the same conference, taking the same classes, or reading the same books, you will learn to appreciate it. It makes it simple to discuss how to incorporate it into your own success.

Identifying whether something is effective or not is another way to learn together.

They make for excellent mastermind teams. Once you have determined the how, why, when, what, and who your group will consist of, as well as their rules, you can establish the four pillars and begin developing as a unit.

THE FRUIT

The second variable that played an important role in the Parable of the Sower was the seed. Consequently, it is also pertinent to anyone who desires to live a fruitful Christian existence.

Many deductions and applications can be drawn from the concept of the seed. But before we delve into that, let me remind you that in His interpretation, the Lord equated the seed to the word of God. Therefore, every conclusion drawn from the concept of the seed applies to the Word of God.

In the initial stage

"In the beginning, the Word was with God, and the Word was God. He existed in the beginning alongside God. 3 All things were created through Him, and nothing was created apart from Him. 4 In Him was life, and life was mankind's source of illumination." John 1:1-4

The verses above suggest several things about God's word.

According to the Parable of the Sower, thirty, sixty, and one hundredfold harvests began with the planting of seeds. This suggests that seeds are essential for reproduction and growth. They are the process's vitality. Without seedlings, there cannot be any fruitfulness.

Since the Lord Jesus equated the seed to God's word, this implies that God's word precedes the advent of all things. It is the instrument for efficiency and fruitfulness.

God does nothing or participates in nothing without first declaring it through His word. Therefore, the phrase "and God said" is conspicuous in Genesis, the book of origins. There was nothing that came into existence that God did not command or declare prior to its occurrence. Thus, the word of God is God's standard operating system and the source of all of God's actions.

God is the Holy Spirit. Only through the manifestation of His words do we observe Him in action. He speaks, then performs the action. And when we observe the fulfillment of His words, we recognize that God is at work. He interacts with us through His words. The word of God is the basis for any step, movement, or idea that will have an impact and significance in God's dominion. It is the outset of everything of significance in God's realm. God creates things with His word.

If we are to ever be productive and successful in God's dominion, our journey must begin with His word. Whatever we desire from God will only occur through His word. His words are the agents of change. God does not create ideas, strategies, or philosophies that do not commence with the word.

It is fine to have ambitions and desires, but if they are not birthed by the word of God, they are irrelevant to God, even if they see the light of day.

"The word was with God in the beginning..." This statement implies that we must have God's approval before undertaking anything of significance in life. It is not simply a word, but a word from God. Therefore, the pursuance of God's word should be a man's top priority in all endeavors.

The instrument for productivity and growth in the hands of the sower is the seed. In fact, a sower cannot be considered a sower if he lacks seeds to cultivate. The fact that a sower has seeds to sow is what makes him a sower. Similarly, the word of God is essential for believers who seek influence and growth.

As an entrepreneur, the first resource you need is God's word. As a minister of the gospel, you should prioritize hearing from God before engaging in ministry. Securing God's word is equivalent to securing God's strength, honor, support, and commitment. God does not commit to anything that does not involve His word. God's Word is your genuine insurance policy for your business, church, ministry, enterprise, or idea.

Therefore, it should be the very first item you secure prior to anything else.

If you want to experience kingdom-relevant growth, you must be able to say this about every action, innovation, business, ambition, and strategy.

The Word Is Vital

Life is a quality you will not find in your human growth and expansion ideas, philosophies, and strategies. This attribute is unique to God's revelation.

"It is the spirit that gives life; the flesh profits nothing; and the words that I speak to you are spirit and life." John 6:63.

Note that Jesus calls the very words He speaks Spirit and Life in the verse above! This implies that God's word lends life and spirit to everything we do in life. Any church that lacks God's word is lifeless. Every concept, goal, and endeavor that is not conceived and sustained by God's word is lifeless. It may be successful in the corporeal world, but it will ultimately amount to nothing and perish along with the world. Anything with eternal characteristics and significance must have vitality and life.

According to the Bible, "As the body without the spirit is dead, so faith without deeds is also dead." The body without the spirit is lifeless (James 2:26). Everything else we do is symbolic of the body. It is God's word that supports those elements that give it a spiritual (life) dimension. The word of God imparts spirit and vitality to everything we do.

While it is necessary to take all the actions, develop the vision and mission statements, and devise all the strategies that will help us achieve our goals, we must not get carried away with them. We must remember that faith precedes action, not the other way around. The Bible does not state that deeds are without faith; rather, it states that faith is without deeds. This implies that faith is required prior to taking action. In actuality, your actions should be motivated by your faith. It is actions that complement faith, not faith that complements actions.

However, the only source of faith is God's word. "Therefore, faith comes through hearing, and hearing through God's word." Romans 10:17

Any action or step we take apart from God's word is not an act of faith, but a risk. You cannot claim to have faith if you have never heard the word.

Chapter 4: The Word Is A Source Of Illumination.

The idiom "God's word is a lamp unto my feet" is a figure of speech intended to emphasize the wisdom contained in God's word. This verse supports the notion that the only sure path to godly wisdom and comprehension is to rely on God's word.

In society, lamps are used to create illumination for movement and activity. Niyr is the Hebrew term for lamp. This description of a lamp more closely resembles the soft glow of a candle. The implication is that visibility of the adjacent area is limited, but there is sufficient light for navigation. The word illuminates your path. It provides step-by-step instructions for attaining God's will for your existence. Even in the harshest environments, it is possible to progress in life if you have sufficient illumination.

These directions culminate in what we refer to as insight. The Bible states that guiding with wisdom is profitable. The pattern and direction for our daily activities are established by God's word. It informs what we should and should not do. God's word provides us with vision and aspiration, and this applies to all aspects of existence.

God's lamp does not disclose the future in its entirety. However, our effectiveness in living according to God's word is not dependent on how far ahead we can see. It depends on our relationship with God.

The Word imparts optimism

No one genuinely lacks noble goals and aspirations in life. Everyone desires success and greatness in life. Every church desires to develop and expand the boundaries of God's kingdom.

It is not a lack of ambition and desire that prevents many individuals from attaining greatness in life; rather, it is life itself. What do I mean when I say that "life happens to them"? I mean that the difficulties, atrocities, and vicissitudes of life demoralize many individuals to the point where they lose faith in their ambition. Life presents them with an unforeseen circumstance. Consequently, they abandon hope.

And because we live in a world that is self-destructing, the majority of the messages we imbibe focus on evil and its manifestations. As our minds absorb these messages from the outside world, even devotees can succumb to doubt and panic.

Possibly you are stating that I will not lose faith. I commend your courage! However, be cautious, comrade. In a world with so many obstacles and atrocities, it is simple to lose hope. Fear and despair are human traits. These are our default settings, which are vexing remnants of our previous nature.

The only source of faith we have is the Bible. The Bible gives us access to liberating truths that can restore our pleasure at any time. The only thing that can sustain our hope is God's word, because we know it will certainly come to pass. The only thing God guarantees will occur despite the difficulties of this world is His word.

"You are my hiding place and my shield; I put my hope in your word" (Psalm 119:114 ESV).

Those whose hope is not in God's word are destined to abandon hope. If your optimism for growth and expansion is not grounded in the Bible, you will eventually lose that hope. The word of God is what gives our aspirations and expectations life and substance. You cannot be certain of accomplishing anything in your life that is not supported by the Bible.

If you have God's word, even if life's storms seem to overwhelm you, there is still a glimmer of promise because God has spoken to you. And since God's word must be fulfilled, this can give you hope that you will prevail. In times of difficulty, the word of God energises and motivates us. Even in dismal situations, the possessor of God's word has hope.

In the same way that the seed in the sower's hand gives him hope that he can propagate that fruit, the word of God gives those who have it hope that it is not yet over.

2. Utilize Productivity Tools

There are innumerable digital and non-digital productivity tools. If you want to be productive and stay on track with all of your work tasks, you must ensure that you are utilizing them. You can use written organizational methods such as planners and desk calendars if you lack technological expertise.

These are ideal for those who prefer to write by hand rather than type on a computer. Simply remember to carry your planner with you when you are at work or making appointments.

If you are organizing with non-digital tools, you may also wish to use colorful pens or adhesive notes. Different colors can also be used to differentiate between work, school, and personal duties.

Those who are immersed in the digital world for work or personal interests may find it more convenient to maintain everything digital, since they almost always have access to a computer. Your computer, smartphone, and tablet all have excellent organizational and productivity tools. Most of them are gratis, allowing for simple verification.

As with non-digital tools, you need a calendar to monitor your responsibilities. The benefit of going digital is that they can be synchronized from one device to another. This enables access to your calendar from your smartphone, smartwatch, computer, and tablet.

If you have separate digital devices for business and personal use, you can keep them distinct by only syncing work-related devices with other work-related devices. This enables you to maintain a separation between work and personal life, which can significantly increase your productivity.

3. Don't Resist Change

People's unwillingness to make changes in their lives is a major factor in their inability to be productive. Changing a routine, an employment, or many other aspects of life can be difficult because it requires letting go and leaving your comfort zone.

Nonetheless, if you are struggling with productivity, something in your life must alter so that you can form new habits. It is perfectly acceptable and normal to be apprehensive about undergoing a radical life transformation.

Try making only one change at a time. Once you have adjusted to the transition, you can move on to something else. In order to ease into your new lifestyle, you can also begin with a minor adjustment.

4. Take frequent breaks during the day

Every time you labor, you must take a break to regain your focus and maintain your energy. However, breaks are not only required for employment. If you are working on a project or practicing a hobby at home, you must also take pauses.

The Pomodoro method is a popular technique used by many. It has been shown to be effective for many individuals because it provides defined work periods and rest periods. This enables you to have a consistent work and leisure schedule.

Taking a break with a friend or colleague can make it more enjoyable. Attempt to do something active during your break, such as stretching or strolling around the office. You can also use this time to quickly refuel with a cup of coffee or a protein sustenance.

This affords you ample time for relaxation and recharging. If you do not wish to use the Pomodoro technique, you can always take breaks as you complete duties. However, in order to avoid rushing through lengthy duties, it may be necessary to divide them into sections.

5. Perform the Most Difficult Tasks First

As the day progresses and you approach your departure time, you may become less and less productive. Therefore, it is recommended that you complete the most difficult duties in the morning, when you have a full day ahead of you and are at your most productive.

You may also want to complete the task you detest the most first thing in the morning. This allows you to get it out of the way and provides you with a sense of accomplishment that you can carry throughout the remainder of the day as you complete additional tasks on your to-do list.

6. Get Adequate Rest

According to some, slumber is the greatest obstacle to productivity. If you aren't getting enough sleep or aren't sleeping well, you'll have trouble focusing on the duties at hand for the remainder of the day. Without vitality and motivation, the remainder of the day is doomed to failure.

If you have difficulty sleeping, you may need to make some changes to your lifestyle so that you expend more energy during the day and sleep better at night. You could also try meditating or drinking tea before slumber.

If you're curious about how much or how well you sleep, you can use a variety of apps to monitor your sleeping. They can also see how often you enter REM sleep, which provides additional information about the quality of your sleep.

7. Begin with the Right Attitude

When it comes to productivity, it is essential to have the proper mindset. Some days will be more difficult than others to alter your mindset, but you should strive to have a positive outlook every morning. Your intellect is your greatest asset in terms of becoming more productive.

Your mind can easily convince you to delay or postpone actions until tomorrow. Learning how to counteract such beliefs can be your greatest obstacle. However, your mind is also capable of reassuring you that you are capable of more and that you can persevere even when circumstances appear difficult.

A positive mental attitude can set you up for success and boost your productivity. Mindfulness practice and mental exercises will guarantee a change in perspective. One method that people practice mindfulness throughout the day is through meditation. There may not be a place to sit and meditate in your office, but you can always meditate before and after work at home.

Throughout the workday, you can take a few pauses and breaks to assess your progress and ensure that you are proceeding in the correct direction. Additionally, meditation has numerous health benefits, such as reducing tension, lowering blood pressure, and promoting homeostasis in the body. It can even reduce stress hormones such as cortisol in the body.

Even if you are not meditating, you can still practice thorough breathing at work. Try taking some deep breaths at your workstation while at work. You can exercise better breathing at home while performing yoga or working out. Try some slow yoga to get your respiration under control.

Chapter 5: You Are Able To Accomplish The Unthinkable.

If you've ever had a plethora of tasks to complete or tasks that seemed beyond your abilities, you know what it's like to feel as though it's impossible. When these kinds of responsibilities fall under your purview, you can employ a variety of beneficial strategies. You may discover that you are capable of accomplishing the seemingly insurmountable.

Due to the overwhelming quantity of work you must complete in a short period of time, you may occasionally view projects as impossible. Even though these are all relatively simple tasks, they may add up to an insurmountable quantity of work that you cannot possibly complete. This could occur if you accept more responsibilities than you can manage, or if unexpected "surprises" occur.

In the first scenario, being realistic about what you can accomplish initially is an effective strategy. This issue can be resolved by assessing your capabilities beforehand, regardless of whether taking on too much is a result of financial necessity, a desire to impress your boss or outdo a colleague, or a failure to consider things through before accepting each responsibility. Learning how to prioritize is an effective strategy for handling the second scenario. Determine which tasks must be completed immediately and which can wait if an unexpected assignment or project arises while you are completing your other responsibilities. Generally, it makes sense to request additional time to complete tasks.

Occasionally, you may be working on an endeavor that is beyond your capabilities. The wisest course of action in these circumstances is to recognize your limitations. Depending on the circumstances, you can either declare that you are unable to perform the task or request assistance.

Achieving the impossible requires efficient time management and a firm grasp of one's capabilities. As a result, your energy and self-esteem will increase, as opposed to being depleted by work or fretting yourself sick about something you cannot do. You will act to the best of your ability, despite the fact that nobody can accomplish or do everything perfectly. Consequently, you will feel less encumbered and be able to work much more effectively.

Don't Let Setbacks Depress You!

A typical reaction to setbacks is one of the greatest impediments to productivity. If you interpret a setback as a failure, it can decrease your productivity and even prevent you from taking any action. This is true in any profession, academic environment, or other aspect of life. If you interpret a setback as a failure, it can prohibit you from progressing. You may accomplish less, or you may accomplish nothing at all.

Setbacks occur in all facets of existence. Regardless of your occupation, you likely encounter them occasionally or frequently. One can experience setbacks as a result of making errors, being unprepared for the tasks at hand, or encountering unavoidable problems.

Your perception of a setback will determine how it affects you and your output.

There is always a perspective that can prevent a setback from becoming an obstacle and even increase productivity. Refusing to view the setback as a failure is the first step toward regaining your footing, regardless of whether it was your fault or someone else's.

The following phase is to view failure as an opportunity to improve the situation in the future. If you uncover an error in your work, you should attempt to correct it before continuing. You must not attempt to conceal an error, but you must also not let an error cause you to cease. If you do not resolve it and move on, you may find yourself dwelling on it.

You may scold yourself for committing the error or become obsessed with it. These actions never yield positive results. In addition to hindering your productivity, they will also make you feel self-conscious. At its worst, it may render you helpless. This is not the proper way to conduct business.

A far superior approach is to view each setback as a learning opportunity. You are capable of convincing yourself that you can perform duties more effectively and efficiently. If you view setbacks in this manner rather than as failures, they will not impede your progress. Correct the error, observe the lesson, and proceed. Once you have established this pattern and made it a normal part of your working life, setbacks will no longer hinder your productivity.

Chapter 6: Effective Productivity Routines

As intriguing as the concept of multitasking may sound, it is not an effective method for achieving optimum productivity. We are humans, not machines. Computers were designed to perform multiple operations simultaneously and produce results almost immediately. We were created somewhat differently. We were designed to take a more in-depth approach in order to achieve extraordinary results. We have been designed for concentration and focus. In our circumstance, garbage-in, garbage-out is not applicable. We need to be thoughtful and patient.

If you have several duties outlined for the day, do not attempt to complete them simultaneously. Best practice suggests that you should complete one task before moving on to the next. Thus, you will accomplish more and produce superior results.

Overburdening your mind with too many tasks will leave you exhausted and unable to complete additional tasks. A solitary completed task is preferable to multiple unfinished ones.

Close the mailbox: I understand that this may sound completely impossible in our current social networking culture. Everyone always appears to be busy on the internet, responding to emails and communicating with friends and coworkers via various chatting applications and websites. Despite the fact that some of these activities may be part of our most essential daily responsibilities, they can be extremely disruptive to our productivity. They consume so much of our time that we are oblivious to the amount of time we devote to them.

More often than not, the majority of these messages do not necessarily move us closer to our intended objectives. Keep in mind that you cannot control time; you can only control yourself. Consequently, time management is life management (Brian Tracy).Setting specific times per day for replying to messages is a strategic method to ensure that your inbox does not consume too much of your time. This may occur in the morning and evening, afternoon and evening, or at your discretion. Say 9:45 to 10 a.m. in the morning and 8 to 9 p.m. in the evening. This plan will save you a significant amount of time and increase your productivity. App alarms on your mobile device can also help you save more time each day (I will provide a list of excellent options at the end of this article).

Eliminate distractions: Distractions are not planned for. They just pop up and steal our attention away. Highly productive people know the danger of unwarranted distractions and take decisive steps to shut them out completely. It could come in form of sitting in a noisy environment or simply receiving a phone call. Let's put it straight, distractions are distractions no matter how we try to paint them. Sometimes we even give excuses to ourselves to justify what obviously are distractions.

The solution to distraction is very easy- simply eliminate them. Yes, you read that clearly. Don't give distractions a breathing space. If you need to put on your head phones to maintain focus then do it. If you have to leave that conversation with your colleague in the office/work place which is gradually becoming a press conference, then do so. Above all, be sensitive to things that seem justifiable but in the long run do not drive you towards achieving your set targets. Do well to dismiss or walk away from them. You will be saving yourself a lot of energy for more relevant work.

Don't be discouraged by defeat; failure is not inherently negative. It is your response to failure that determines the course of your existence. Failure should be viewed as a launching stone to greater success. Don't become trapped because of a single setback. Successful individuals fail, but what they do with their failures is what sets them apart. They recognize that failure is not fatal, which is why they get back up after each tumble. They never remain stationary for too long. You are only vanquished when you allow your most recent setback to determine your fate. Instead of being afraid of making errors, view failure as an opportunity for growth.

Small movements are just as significant as large ones. Every successful undertaking begins with a concept. Beginning a lengthy voyage always begins with a single step. The most intelligent employees break down enormous tasks into small, manageable steps and then tackle them piece by piece. Numerous individuals struggle with the desire to take on everything at once. This practice severely hinders productivity. It is the same as attempting to lose the calories that would normally be lost in two months of regular exercise in a single day or attempting to memorize a thousand pages of course material in a few days before an exam. Or perhaps you want to construct a duplex in three days (strange, right?). Lol). These scenarios are impractical because everything of enduring value requires time to construct. Therefore, do not hurry. Build incrementally and one step at a time.

Making the most of your morning hours can be one of the finest decisions you ever make in terms of maximizing your productivity. Those few hours before the rest of the world awakens may be all you need to gain an advantage. According to studies, your willpower and creativity are at their peak in the morning. Most successful people subscribe to the technique of maximizing the few early hours of the day before dawn. It functions. There are fewer distractions, allowing you to concentrate and accomplish more. You should utilize these early hours to set the tone for the remainder of the day.

Eating the frog refers to completing the most difficult duty of the day first thing in the morning. Mark Twain is famous for his proverb, "If you eat a live frog in the morning, the rest of the day will be uneventful."
This is a very powerful statement because we frequently fail to complete the most essential task of the day by the end of the day. Why is this occurring? Why don't we complete them eventually? The answer is

straightforward: we let them sit for too long. We don't confront them head-on at the beginning of the day, and this has prevented us from making significant progress. We repeatedly neglect deadlines and only offer apologies.

If you truly believe that this task is crucial, you should complete it first thing in the morning. Don't keep it waiting for so long. You'll be amazed at how easy the remainder of the day is if you attack it head-on at the beginning of the day. Once the day's most important task has been completed, the remainder of the day's tasks appear extremely simple. Suppose, for instance, that you find doing your laundry to be extremely difficult. Instead of postponing your laundry until the evening, why not "eat that frog" as soon as you wake up? Perform the task immediately. You will realize how fulfilled you are by the end of the day. I can attest to the efficacy of this technique, as I've used it repeatedly. It functions very well.

Eat Wisely: What you eat and don't ingest directly impacts your ability to be productive. The World Health Organization (WHO) estimates that consuming the proper foods can increase cognitive function by up to 20%. dining regularly is not equivalent to dining regularly and healthily. Repeat the reading! Select your nutrients carefully. Do not believe that anything is acceptable as long as it is sustenance. You can conduct research on which food components are useful for accomplishing specific duties. This will serve as your guide to developing healthful eating habits that will increase your overall productivity. Avoid high-fat and high-sugar meals, which can cause you to collapse and impair your productivity. You don't want to go through the day with a fatigued and muddled mind and accomplish nothing. This is why you must select your menu with care and delicacy.

Plan your day the night before: Frequently, I am preoccupied with how taxing the following day will be. Occasionally, I go to bed distressed and lose quality sleep. Perhaps you do the same. It is not a terrible idea to think about the next day, but it is a bad idea to let that thought drain you before the next day arrives. What you should be doing instead is taking time to organize your day. The most productive employees prepare their morning schedules the night before. Taking a few minutes before bed to organize your tasks for the following day will give you clarity and confidence to tackle the day. It reduces anxiety and apprehension. It provides you the confidence to face the day because you feel like you have everything under control. We humans dislike being in uncertain circumstances. We enjoy having everything sorted out. Before taking the next step, we want to be certain of its purpose. If you devote 20 minutes at night to planning your day, you will be better prepared when the next day approaches.

Utilize productivity applications: we inhabit a technologically-driven ecosystem. You and I have access to tens of thousands of ingenious productivity-enhancing applications. Why wouldn't you utilize the most effective resources available to you? Utilize cutting-edge technology to give yourself a fair (not unjust) advantage and observe the results you achieve. Remember that productivity is the capacity to produce substantial results. Whatever works well for you should be utilized to the fullest extent possible. Utilizing technology will change the situation for you. You will accomplish more and save valuable time.

If you want to increase your productivity, you should run. Highly productive individuals place exercise near the summit of their to-do list. Exercise can aid in reducing tension and significantly enhancing your mood. It has the capacity to improve memory, attention span, and creativity. Morning is the optimal time for exercising. Establishing a regular exercise regimen will significantly enhance your productivity. In comparison to those who do not take exercise seriously, your mind is clear and you are able to generate solutions and ideas swiftly and accurately.

If you own a business or are an employer, you may need to delegate tasks. Keeping the large picture in mind at all times is your sole responsibility. You have so much on your mind that you must ensure that everything runs efficiently. This motivates you to be in control of every situation. You want to partake in doing everything possible, either because you genuinely enjoy your work, because you want to demonstrate to your employees how hard you work, or because you are a workaholic. It must be one of these three options. You eventually exert yourself to the point of utter exhaustion. You may not realize how gravely this is affecting your productivity, but it is. You are presumably completely obsessed with the outcomes you seek.

God bless you for reading this now. Please cease! You do not have to complete every task by yourself. You do not have to carry the entire weight of your enterprise on your own shoulders. If another person is more qualified for a task, delegate it. Delegating tasks not only helps you maintain focus on the big picture, but it also improves the confidence and skill sets of your team members. If you ask me what the simplest method is to help your employees develop competence, I'll say delegating tasks to them. It does work.

You will progressively instill confidence and competence in those around you if you delegate tasks intelligently and provide a deadline. They will appreciate it, and you will further establish their trust.

Learn to say 'no': This is where many individuals who desire productivity go terribly awry. It is not a crime to occasionally deny inquiries from other individuals. Attempting to accommodate everyone's needs at the expense of your own schedule is detrimental to your productivity. Successful individuals recognize the importance of their time and place a premium on it. Time is an extremely valuable resource. It is the most valuable resource on the planet. Learn to say no occasionally when something is completely inconvenient. For instance, you are occupied at work when a coworker requests your assistance with a task. If you legitimately cannot spare the time, politely decline with explanation. You don't have to do so in an impolite or dismissive manner; simply explain your situation and, if possible, suggest an alternative source of assistance. They will comprehend and value your recommendation. If you genuinely want to be productive, you must place a high value on your time, as it cannot be recovered.

Utilize the most effective short-cuts when necessary. In order to be truly effective, it is sometimes necessary to take the shortest route to achieve results. You have no reason to feel guilty for taking short routes. As long as it does not negatively affect the outcome of your endeavor. You should only use a short cut when doing so has no impact on the grade of your results. Shortcuts are a significant time saver. Why, for example, should you take the longer route to work if there is a shorter route? As long as you will achieve the same outcome (going to work) but much more quickly, you should take the quickest route to work.

Always ask more seasoned professionals in your field about the techniques they use to accomplish more and save time for other tasks. You may discover just how much tension you've been under all along. I have previously discussed utilizing technology. If you knew the shortcuts, you could accomplish so much in a brief amount of time. And you can learn about them by inquiring.

Eliminate unimportant tasks: "Deciding what not to do is just as important as deciding what to do"

Once you have a firm grasp of this, you have taken a clear step in the correct direction toward becoming incredibly productive. Learning to identify non-essential duties is a crucial skill for anyone who wants to be effective. We are oblivious to the nature of these trivial responsibilities. They are always camouflaged as time-consuming endeavors, but in reality, they are not as important as they appear. Ask yourself: Is a 45-minute meeting with your team members truly necessary? If the answer is 'no', terminate the meeting or, better yet, reduce it to 15 minutes in order to save more time for actual work. If your day contains unnecessary administration and bureaucracy, eliminate them. The majority of the time, we engage in time-wasting activities merely out of habit, not because they serve any meaningful purpose.

Setting clearly defined goals is essential if you hope to ever reach your objectives. Clarify your objectives completely. Effective goal setting does not permit any assumptions. Be sincere and realistic, first with yourself and then with others. Don't over-estimate your abilities. This will only result in self-sabotage and further frustration with your own efforts.

Set a deadline for your goals and find a partner for accountability. Setting a deadline for your goals is just as essential as setting clearly defined ones. Adding a deadline to your objectives is important because it keeps you on your toes until all of the boxes are checked. You should also have a partner who will keep you disciplined. Having someone or a group to whom you are accountable is an excellent method to maintain focus. It is in our nature to exert additional effort when we are held accountable for something; particularly when we hold the person in question in such high regard and do not wish to disappoint them. We would do whatever it takes to complete the task because we don't want to be reprimanded by someone we respect for missing a goal. This natural environment can be utilized to increase productivity.

Examine and know your optimal environment: There is an optimal environment for each individual. Your optimal environment is any condition that optimizes your efficiency and output. Do you work more effectively in an office or a coffee shop? Yours is possibly even at home. Determine your optimal environment by observing your reaction to various settings. You do not need to conform to society's standards. If you are unable to achieve optimal results due to your current environment, you should request a change. If there is a significant difference and increase in your productivity after a change of environment, you will likely be permitted to work in your preferred space more often.

After the global lockdown in 2020, many businesses granted the requests of certain employees to continue working from home, as their productivity had skyrocketed during the lockdown. Even after the lockdown, tech companies such as Facebook, Spotify, and Twitter are progressively shifting toward remote work on a long-term basis. Mark Zuckerberg, the founder and chief executive officer of Facebook, wrote: "Working remotely has given me more time for long-term planning and allowed me to spend more time with my family, which has made me happier and more productive at work." In addition, he anticipates that approximately half of Facebook's employees will work remotely within the next decade (source: Chicagobooth.edu).

This is the opinion of a highly successful entrepreneur, which is shared by a large number of individuals. If, on the other hand, you are the type of person who would not dare work from home due to distractions, but prefers the office culture, then you should always be in the office. Even though working from home is advantageous for Zuckerberg, not everyone shares his perspective. In other interviews, corporations such as JPMorgan Chase and Goldman Sachs preferred the 'tried-and-true' office setting. David Solomon, chief executive officer of Goldman Sachs, described working from home as "an anomaly that must be rectified as soon as possible." The CEO of JPMorgan, Jamie Dimon, had this to say about remote work: "It doesn't work for those who are ambitious. It does not work for generating spontaneous ideas. It is ineffective for culture".

What exactly am I advocating? I want you to observe how the leaders of various prominent, successful companies have diverse perspectives on the workplace. The point is to know where you succeed. Determine and adhere to the environment that promotes your productivity the most. Some tasks, however, cannot be performed remotely because they require human interaction, or the requisite technology has not yet been developed. In such a scenario, employees are required to be physically available. If this describes you, you should make every effort to modify your work environment so that you can be more productive.

Recognize the need for breaks and rest: Understanding when to take genuine rest breaks is crucial to being productive. Everyone has a maximum level of tension that their bodies can tolerate. Exceeding this peak will only result in disintegration and poor performance, which will eventually lead to low productivity. Resting when necessary has a significant impact on both your physical health and your level of productivity. Take a break when you anticipate reaching the climax, as this may be all you need to give your finest performance.

Prioritize Your Objectives

Every objective that you set will be challenging, as they all require dedication and consistent effort. Therefore, do not undermine yourself by pursuing multiple objectives simultaneously. I would recommend focusing on no more than three goals at once, and even then, you should choose one as your top priority. This recommendation is based on the assumption that you are adhering to all of the other goal-setting advice presented in this article and that you know how to set worthwhile goals.

Realize Your Goals to Yourself

Essentially, goal setting is a method for approaching the process of accomplishment. It is a highly effective method if executed properly, but, as with all such methods, it is somewhat ethereal. Using techniques such as visualization to concentrate on what actually achieving your goal will feel like and what it will do for you can be extremely effective - and a great motivational tool. Choosing and posting images that represent the accomplishment of your objective is another method for achieving this.

Establish Deadlines to Achieve Your Objectives

A goal without a deadline is a goal to which you have not completely committed and will not be attained. Firstly, if working towards an objective is something that can be done whenever, you won't. In addition, having a deadline will define your strategy. To return to the debt illustration, it makes a significant difference whether your objective is to be debt-free in two or five years. Clearly, you will need to drastically reduce your expenditures or increase your income to pay off your debts faster.

Evaluate Your Goals

Remember that goal setting is a process, and that evaluation is a crucial component of that process. Don't simply accept a 'good' or 'poor' evaluation; consider what you did, how you did it, and what you gained. Whether you achieved your goal successfully or not, there is always something to be learned; what works or doesn't work for you, whether attaining your goal met your expectations, and why you failed. When you implement these lessons to your future goal-setting experience, you will increase your achievements even further.

Reward Yourself for Your Success

Internal satisfaction is wonderful, but external rewards can also be extremely gratifying. When you achieve an objective, you have devoted time and effort to your success; therefore, you should also take the time to celebrate your achievement. One caution: do not undermine your efforts by selecting an unsuitable reward. A new attire, rather than a large slice of cheesecake, would be a more appropriate reward for losing 20 pounds. To achieve your goal, you must first establish one. It makes sense, doesn't it?... Therefore, grab a notebook and a pen and begin writing down your desired goals. Once you have completed this step, you can return to this book and move on to the next chapter, in which I will explain in detail how to construct plans in order to achieve your desired outcomes.

2

Consider the Time Required to Achieve the Objective.

Setting specific deadlines will help you remain organized and on track to achieve your goals. This method is very useful when you need to effectively manage your time while working on multiple tasks simultaneously. In addition to aiding in time management, deadlines enable you to hold yourself accountable for achieving your objectives. You can stay organized and on schedule to achieve your objectives by breaking down and assigning due dates to your larger objectives.

Using the created time frames, indicate on each target destination sheet the year you will complete the objective.

Consider the deadline you would like to achieve for any objective without a fixed end date, and use that as your destination date.

At this juncture, the five-year, ten-year, and next-year plans enter the picture.

Recognize the differences between short-term and long-term goals. Due to age, health, finances, etc., certain objectives will have a "shelf life." Others will be your responsibility to complete by your chosen deadline.

Work within the constraints of each goal's deadline and record the dates by which each of the lesser tasks will be completed.

4. List the actions required to attain each objective.

To accomplish your objective, list the steps you must take to complete each of the given items, one after the other.

These items will be added to an inventory. They offer a concrete way to evaluate your progress towards attaining your goals. A listing of your achievements

5. Organize Your Task List

After taking stock of all of your objective locations, create a calendar of the tasks you must complete this week, this month, or this year in order to make progress toward your goals.

If you record these action items on a schedule, you have specific deadlines for completing them.

6. Evaluate Your Development

Review your accomplishments at the end of the year, remove items from your to-do lists for each objective location, and construct a plan with the necessary action steps for the following year.

You will ultimately be successful in reaching your goal destination because you have planned out not only what you want, but also how to get it, and have been proactive towards achieving it, even though it may take you several years to, for instance, get the promotion you desire because you first need to obtain an MBA, which necessitates obtaining a higher-paying job in order to finance a part-time degree program.

Analysis paralysis

Analysis paralysis is the second negative consequence of information overload that is more specific to technical professionals. Extremely lengthy phases of project planning, requirements collection, and data modeling are typical manifestations of this issue in software development.

Those acquainted with agile software development may be familiar with this anti-pattern example. In fact, agile development explicitly aims to avoid analysis paralysis by promoting an iterative work cycle that places a premium on functional products rather than product specifications.

Now that we've experienced all the difficulties that information overload causes, we must concentrate on coping with it. I will provide five solutions for this.

Brain Dump

This is actually more of a practice session. You must compose an inventory of all the thoughts that are currently running through your mind. Therefore, halt for a moment and write down everything that is on your mind. Everything, including every task, to-do, problem, and business transaction. This should require several minutes.

Done?

Perfect.

Now, you must determine an exact completion date for each item on the list, or simply remove it from the list. If you were offered a business venture, either embrace it and get the ball rolling or let the other party know that you are not interested at this time.

Having 100 items in the "someday" category is a waste of mental and physical resources and will hinder your ability to concentrate.

The Rule of Two Minutes

The two-minute rule is the second method for coping with information overload. It is necessary to divide your duties into these two categories. There are activities that require more than two minutes and those that require less. Then, group these small duties together and complete them in a condensed period of time. If you continue to alternate between these larger and smaller duties, they will take 10 minutes. Additionally, transferring your attention frequently from one task to another will hinder your productivity. Therefore, it is essential to focus on one at a time.

Prioritizing Important Decisions

The third strategy for managing information inundation is to prioritize the most crucial decisions first. In the preceding section, I discussed prioritizing duties, but I would like to share another perspective on this topic.

Kelly McGonigal explains in her book The Willpower Instinct that willpower is a limited resource. Therefore, if you use it on trivial decisions and duties when faced with crucial ones, you may run out. Therefore, it is essential to begin with the most crucial tasks.

Numerous businesses use this data to determine that your willpower is a limited resource. The placement of products in supermarkets to maximize profits is evident on a daily basis. There is an entire science behind product placement, including structure files, what appears at eye level and what does not, pricing, and even the soundtrack.

Control Authority

The fourth method for coping with information overload is delegated authority, which is extremely useful for managers. It's essentially a delegation of stewardship. You delegate in such a way that the individuals you manage comprehend the project objective, so you do not need to review their methods; instead, you analyze the results.

Turning Off Things

Turning things off is the last and sometimes most difficult solution to information inundation. Without an emitter, it is impossible to be overwhelmed with data. Therefore, disable phone notifications that interrupt applications. Close the television and radio and, most crucially, keep your email tab open.

And, if you use even one of these techniques, you will observe significant improvements in your ability to deal with information overload and in your speed of decision-making.

In the following subsection, we will discuss the issue that affects the majority of us. It's a case of procrastination. But despite knowing what you must do and why you must do it, you put it off until the last minute. And if you have this issue, I trust the next section will help you combat procrastination and finally complete that project you've been putting off.

www.ingramcontent.com/pod-product-compliance
Lightning Source LLC
Chambersburg PA
CBHW070309120526
44590CB00017B/2607